Gorillas
For Kids

Amazing Animal Books
For Young Readers

By
Rachel Smith

Mendon Cottage Books
JD-Biz Corp Publishing

Read More Amazing Animal Books

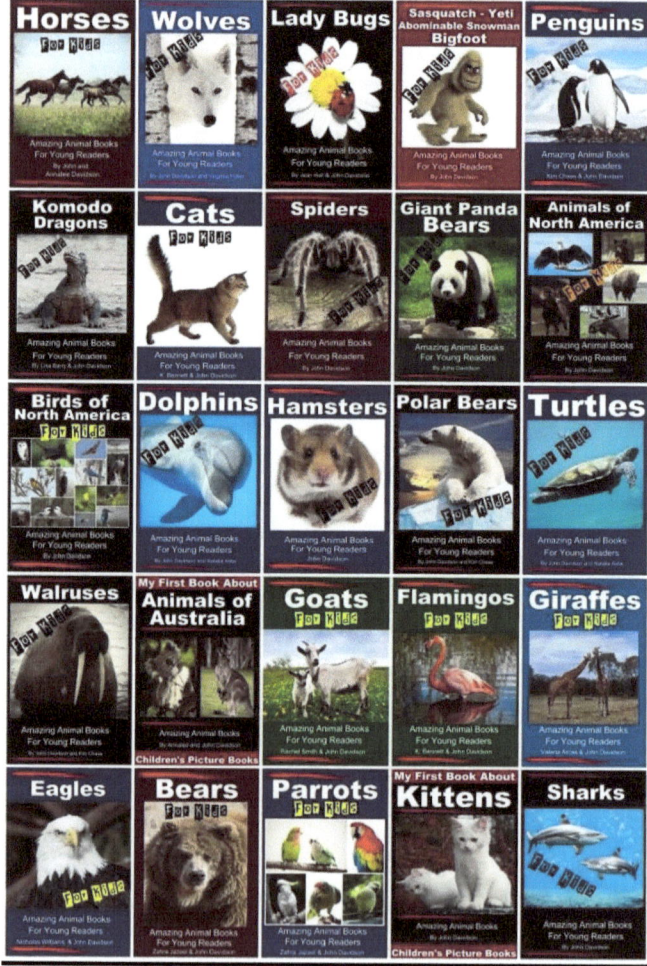

Table of Contents

Introduction 4

What is a gorilla? 5

What kinds of gorillas are there? 10

The history of gorillas and humans 12

Cross River Gorilla 15

Western Lowland Gorilla 18

Eastern Lowland Gorilla 21

Mountain Gorilla 23

Conclusion 25

Author Bio 26

Publisher 27

Introduction

Gorillas have long interested people. When the large apes were discovered by Europeans, it sent a frenzy into the scientific community. Never before had such large apes been seen, at least not by them. They were not so unusual to the societies already living in the same general area.

Westerners believed that the gorilla was a violent beast, meat-eating and foul-tempered. They believed this because of the gorilla's teeth, and because most of them only saw dead gorillas, rather than seeing them living in their natural habitat.

The myths and false assumptions about gorillas would not be disproved for a long time, but now we know the gorilla is not only not particularly violent, but also intelligent and capable of being very gentle. These great animals are an amazing part of the many creatures that make up the world.

What is a gorilla?

A gorilla is a member of the genus Gorilla. The gorilla, all kinds, live in central Africa. This means they live in places such as the Democratic Republic of Congo and Rwanda. The two main types, the western and eastern kinds, are separated by the Congo River and its many tributaries; the Congo River is one of the great rivers of the world, and was long a source of transportation for the colonizers of Central Africa.

A baby gorilla.

A gorilla's DNA, that is, deoxyribonucleic acid (which is kind of the blueprints for any creature's body to follow), is very similar to both humans and chimpanzees. However, chimpanzees and humans are a bit closer in DNA matches. There is a small difference between humans and gorillas, nonetheless.

Gorillas can live in high places, such as mountains, or very low places, such as marshes, depending on what kind they are.

The name gorilla actually comes from a pretty ancient word. Way back in 500 BC, a Carthaginian (from Carthage, which was an empire that rivaled Ancient Rome, and which was on the northern coast of Africa) explorer named Hanno encountered a group of 'people.' He described them as having many more females, being very hairy, and as savages. He called these 'people' (which may have been apes, real people, or some other nonhuman group) Gorillae. This name essentially means, 'tribe of hairy women.'

So, when European explorers discovered gorillas, they thought of this tale, and named them gorillas. They may, in fact, be one and the same, but we just don't know.

Gorillas get around by walking on their back feet and the knuckles of their hands. Sometimes, they will stand to walk about, but usually only for very short distances, and in the case of either carrying something or defending themselves.

Gorillas are described as prognathic, which means that their lower jaw (the mandible) sticks out further than their upper jaw (the maxilla). In humans, this is a problem, but in gorillas it's perfectly normal. They have big teeth, and they're pointy too. Because of this, the scientists who examined dead gorillas assumed that they were meat eaters. However, gorillas are herbivores, meaning that they eat plants.

Males can be anywhere from 135 to 180 kilograms. They also are often around the height of human men, though there have been some very big gorillas that surpass that height. Females tend to be half the size of males, weighing around 68 to 113 kilograms. Their arm span, on both counts, is longer than humans'.

Nesting is very important for gorillas. They use them both during the day and at night. Every gorilla makes their own nest on the ground, except for gorilla babies, who sleep in their mother's nest. However, at about three years of age, the baby gorilla will make their own nest, at first close to their mother's and then further away. They are pretty different from other apes, in that they make nests on the ground with whatever tree materials are available; chimpanzees stay in trees.

Gorillas have certain periods used for rest, travel, or eating. The food eaten by the gorilla really depends on what kind of gorilla it is: some eat a lot of fruit, and others eat very little, instead relying on plants and plant parts.

Male gorillas which have completely grown into adults are called silverbacks; this is because they have silver-colored fur on their backs, usually around the hip area.

A silverback is at least twelve years old, and in a troop of gorillas, is often the leader. Sometimes, a troop will have more than one male, but in general, there must always be a male leader. The silverback will protect the females and young gorillas in its troop with its life.

If the silverback dies, then quite often, the females and young gorillas will find another group, all going their own way. Other times, they will stay together, and a silverback will find them.

It's very common for a gorilla of any kind to leave their troop upon adulthood. It doesn't matter if they're male or female; this is the most common way for a gorilla to find their group. A few, however, do stay with the troop they were born in.

There are also blackbacks often in a troop, which are male gorillas between eight and twelve years of age. They obey the silverback, and often work with him to protect the troop.

Females don't always get along with each other in the troop. If they are related through their mother, then they often like each other; if not, they are much more likely to fight. Males often don't really have relationships with each other of any kind, unless they are in an all-male group, which is a bit unusual.

When it comes to the age for child-bearing, females are ready at ten to twelve years. Males are ready to make babies at eleven to thirteen. A female gorilla's pregnancy is not so different from a human's: pregnancy lasts about 8.5 months, and the baby is helpless and vulnerable.

A baby gorilla needs its mother to survive. They are completely weaned at about three years old, and that's when the mother can have another baby; this means that, provided they have a male gorilla to mate with, a female adult gorilla will have a baby about every four years.

Baby gorillas need milk every hour, and when they get a bit older, only once every two hours. Their fathers don't do a lot with them, but they do often help with socializing the baby with other baby gorillas.

Gorillas can communicate through about twenty five different sounds. They are also highly intelligent, able to use and make tools, as well as do things such as learn sign language. Some have also shown a preference for a certain color and there are seemingly cultures built around food preparation in different gorilla groups.

What kinds of gorillas are there?

There are four known types of gorillas. Some say there are five, but that will be explained in a moment.

A female western lowland gorilla with her baby.

First off, there are two species: western gorilla and eastern gorilla. After that, there are two subspecies each.

For the western gorilla, there's the western lowland gorilla and the Cross River gorilla. The western lowland gorilla is the most common gorilla; there are about one hundred thousand in the wild, with a number in zoos. This is often the gorilla people are thinking of when they think of gorillas. As for the Cross River gorilla, it is a type of gorilla that lives near a river called the Cross River. That river is along the Cameroon-Nigeria border; there are very few left, only about two hundred to three hundred.

The eastern gorilla has its two subspecies as well: the eastern lowland gorilla, of which there are about 4,000, is the first one. There are about 24 of them in zoos; like the western lowland gorilla, it lives in lands that are low, the opposite of mountains.

The other kind of eastern gorilla is the mountain gorilla. There are only around 600 left. This kind lives in the mountains, and has a different appearance than its cousin the eastern lowland gorilla. Also, it really doesn't do well in zoos; there are currently none in captivity.

The proposed fifth kind is the Bwindi (which is a national park in Rwanda) population of mountain gorillas. The belief there is that there is a big enough difference to justify calling it its own subspecies. Not a lot is known about them, though it is known that they eat more fruit than their mountain gorilla cousins over in the other area for them, the Virunga Mountains. Bwindi gorillas make up about half of all mountain gorillas left in the world.

The history of gorillas and humans

Gorillas and humans do not have the best history. For starters, humans thought that gorillas were bloodthirsty monsters in the beginning; it was only some time in the twentieth century (the 1900s) that they realized that the gorilla was an herbivorous animal.

A young mountain gorilla in the Bwindi National Park.

The first live gorilla sighting by a Westerner was Paul Du Chaillu when he traveled through the middle part of Africa; this was in 1856 to 1859. Before that, Westerners had collected specimens (dead gorillas and their parts) but had never seen a live gorilla. He brought back dead gorillas for people to look at.

It was a very different time; killing exotic animals to bring them back to 'civilization' was considered normal and even heroic. Explorers brought back new things all the time, and while sometimes they bothered to bring live animals back, if the animal was big or hard to handle, they would simply shoot it and bring its carcass back.

In the 1920s, still the mindset of killing and stuffing a gorilla for science was the norm. Carl Akeley set out about this time to catch and kill one. With him was the writer Mary Bradley; she soon began to write to bring awareness to gorilla conservation, believing that the animal should be preserved and not harmed.

Finally, after World War II, a man set out and actually studied gorillas in their habitat.

The most conclusive study (and the most impactful one too) was by a woman named Dian Fossey. She studied them and then wrote a book that dispelled myths such as the gorilla being violent. Finally the gorilla was understood to be a peaceful creature that would only fight if threatened.

Nowadays, there are a lot of gorillas in zoos. One of the most prominent gorillas is Koko, who doesn't quite live in a zoo, but rather in the care of a great ape language specialist. She is a gorilla that has learned a special version of sign language, called Gorilla Sign Language, or GSL. She can communicate at about the level of a small child. She's also known for having adopted a kitten. Her name, Koko, is short for Hanabiko, and she is a western lowland gorilla.

Human contact with gorillas may have started back when the Carthaginians might have found them. Or, it may have started with the native African peoples surrounding them. Chances are, they saw them first.

Gorillas have been known to show compassion towards some humans; for instance, Koko was shown to be sad about a caretaker's miscarriage, and gorillas, especially females, have been known to protect small children that have fallen into their exhibits. This is a rare event, so it's not something to assume all gorillas will be friendly small children; they are still wild animals, and some may think humans are threatening them.

Cross River Gorilla

The Cross River gorilla is one of the most endangered in the world. It's also not as widely recognized as its own subspecies as the other three kinds (not counting the Bwindi gorilla).

It was declared its own species in 1904, but it wasn't until 1987 that any surveys of it were done. Thanks to those surveys, we have something of an idea of them, their numbers, and habitat. The Cross River gorilla was only caught on professional video in 2009, showing how behind we are on studying this disappearing creature.

Mostly, they surround the area of the Cross River, a place in Nigeria along the Nigeria-Cameroon border. These are both countries in Africa, towards the center of the continent. It is not as near the Congo River as the other types of gorillas.

The Cross River gorilla is a western gorilla, and while being critically endangered, it doesn't make the top 25 most endangered primates list (a primate is an animal such as a monkey or ape).

It is endangered by forest fires, deforestation, small groups, over-hunting, and limited genetic material. The last one means that they have less variety than most species and other groups, because of there only being about 200-300. This means that they can't help passing on bad genes, and that they can become somewhat inbred, which means the apes are too related to each other.

Cross River gorillas have shorter skulls and various other differences in their skulls from western lowland gorillas. They also have shorter hands, and larger opposable digits (like thumbs) on their feet. Other than that, there's not a very large difference.

It's believed the subspecies developed during the Pleistocene in Africa. Due to changing environment and changing food sources, the Cross River gorilla developed separately from the western lowland gorilla.

Before this, Gorilla gorilla gorilla, the ancestor of the gorillas, was one species. It split into the four a very, very long time ago.

The Cross River gorilla has been known to sometimes defend itself; several have been seen doing things like throwing clumps of grass and sticks at intruders. None have been recorded charging anyone.

Sometimes, Cross River gorillas will build nests in trees instead of on the ground. This seems to depend on both the season and the time of day.

They eat not only mainly fruit, but also things like tree bark. They enjoy leaves of trees and things like that.

The Cross River gorilla is severely endangered. It is also rarely seen, because of its bad experience with hunters. Since hunters are generally human, they avoid all humans if they can.

Western Lowland Gorilla

Western lowland gorillas are the most common kind of gorilla, both in the world and in zoos. This type of gorilla makes a whopping majority of all gorillas in zoos; if you've seen a gorilla in a zoo, it was probably a western lowland gorilla.

A western lowland gorilla; this one's a silverback male.

Despite the name, this kind of gorilla doesn't just live in lowlands. It also often lives in dense forests, somewhat mountainous areas, and other spots. However, it is most often spotted in the lowlands, hence the name.

It is the smallest kind of gorilla. It has jet black skin, coarse hair, and small eyes and nose. Another feature of the western lowland gorilla is the broad, big teeth.

Males and females look different as well. This is called sexual dimorphism, which basically means 'two forms.' The males are a decent amount bigger and taller than the females, and also their heads look different. A female's head is less big.

The reason they use knuckle-walking is because their arm-span is longer than their height; it makes more sense to put them to use this way, with their weight, than it does to drag them along.

One of the enemies of the western lowland gorilla, as well as most gorillas, is the leopard. They may even move their ranges to avoid leopards. Silverbacks have been found dead alongside dead leopards before, showing that both are formidable.

Unlike some animals, the western lowland gorilla is not territorial. A group of gorillas may live in a certain area, but their ranges may overlap, and they won't fight about it. Some animals mark their territory, but gorillas don't do this either.

The western lowland gorilla is endangered, partially due to losing habitat and partially due to being hunted for their skins and meat; this last part is illegal, but it continues in Africa because the people there need to eat. It's a bit more complex than those that hunt gorillas to sell to zoos. That's also illegal, but it goes on.

Another reason these gorillas are hunted by the people who live near and in their habitat is that they tend to raid plantations. Plantations are large sort of farms that grow a crop for money. For instance, they might grow bananas, or cocoa. When gorillas destroy the crops, it makes the people who own them angry, and they want to gorillas gone for that reason.

Eastern Lowland Gorilla

The eastern lowland gorilla is a lot more endangered than the western. However, it is not the most endangered, and still has a good shot at a comeback, having a population of roughly 4,000 left.

An eastern lowland gorilla.

A lot less of these animals are able to be kept in captivity compared with the western lowland gorilla. Only a single female, and some males, are kept in zoos or otherwise. The female is currently in Belgium.

The eastern lowland gorilla is also the largest kind of gorilla. It has thick, jet black fur, though it is much shorter on their body and head as compared to the mountain gorilla.

This type of gorilla needs a lot of food, and they tend to travel in groups like a family to search for more food. Eastern gorilla groups are much bigger than western gorilla groups; they also are less likely to split up temporarily than the western gorillas. Eastern lowland gorillas are very close knit. They also travel less than western gorillas because they eat more foliage (like plants) as opposed to fruit.

The interesting difference between this kind of gorilla's groups and other groups is that often, there will be two silverback males in charge of a group, instead of just one. Also, their group can have as many as 30 gorillas in it.

An eastern lowland gorilla mama may have one baby or twins.

Unfortunately, not a lot is known about the way eastern lowland gorillas live, because for many years now, the place they live, the Democratic Republic of Congo, has been in civil war. It's not the people's fault, because long ago, the Belgians came in and messed everything up under King Leopold II, doing some seriously wrong things to the people who lived there. Because of the Belgians, Congolese people have to deal with the problems that came from them, and right now, the civil war is one of those problems.

Mountain Gorilla

The mountain gorilla is the second-most endangered gorilla, with only a few hundred in existence. None of them live in zoos; people haven't been able to find a way for them to survive and reproduce.

A mountain gorilla in a national park in Rwanda.

Mountain gorillas have jet-black hair all over their bodies, longer hair than the eastern lowland gorilla. They also live in dense forests in mountainous areas. Currently, they live in the Democratic Republic of Congo and Rwanda.

As mentioned before, there has been discussion of the Bwindi population of mountain gorillas actually being a separate species, which would cut the current number in half, but scientists haven't agreed.

Mountain gorillas can live in colder temperatures than other gorillas. Also, they can be individually identified by their nose prints, which are unique to each one.

They have more pronounced bony crests on their skulls, among other differences.

Like the eastern lowland gorilla, they are non-territorial, meaning that they protect their group rather than their land. Most mountain gorillas live in the Virunga Mountains, except for the Bwindi gorilla.

These creatures are generally very gentle and shy; only when their group is threatened do the silverbacks usually fight, and only in unstable groups do other gorillas generally fight.

Conclusion

Gorillas are a national treasure to the countries they live in, but they are disappearing faster than we can imagine. In as little as twenty years, there could be only one or two subspecies left.

Hopefully, we will be able to not only help the gorillas and save them, but help the people who live around them who see no other option than to kill them.

Author Bio

Rachel Smith is a young author who enjoys animals. Once, she had a rabbit which was very nervous, and chewed through her leash and tried to escape. She's also had several pet mice, which were the funniest little animals to watch. She lives in Ohio with her family and writes in her spare time.

Publisher

JD-Biz Corp

P O Box 374

Mendon, Utah 84325

http://www.jd-biz.com/

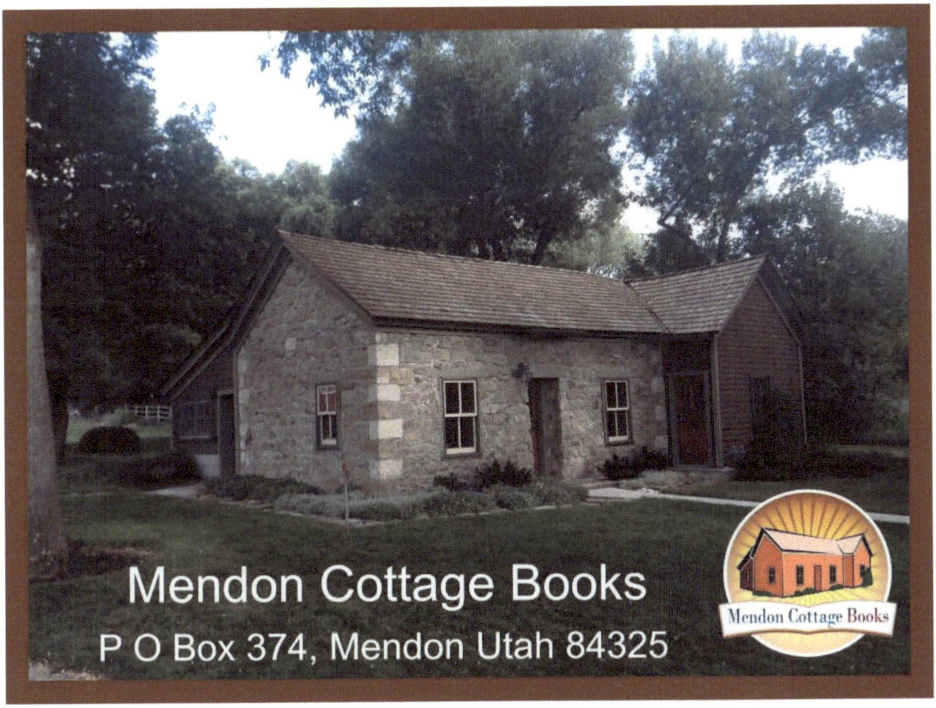

Mendon Cottage Books

P O Box 374, Mendon Utah 84325

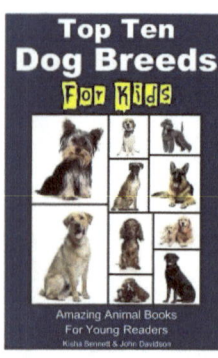

Top Ten Dog Breeds For Kids
Amazing Animal Books For Young Readers
Kisha Bennett & John Davidson

German Shepherds
Dog Books for Kids
K. Bennett

Bulldogs
Dog Books for Kids
K. Bennett

Dachshund
Dog Books for Kids
K. Bennett

Poodles
Dog Books for Kids
K. Bennett

Labrador Retrievers
Dog Books for Kids
K. Bennett

Rottweilers
Dog Books for Kids
K. Bennett

Boxers
Dog Books for Kids
K. Bennett

Golden Retrievers
Dog Books for Kids
K. Bennett

Puppies
Dog Books For Kids
Amazing Animal Books For Young Readers
By John Davidson

Beagles
Dog Books for Kids
K. Bennett

Yorkshire Terriers
Dog Books for Kids
K. Bennett

Dogs
Top Ten Dog Breeds For Kids
Amazing Animal Books For Young Readers
Zahra Jazeel & John Davidson

Cats For Kids
Amazing Animal Books For Young Readers
K. Bennett & John Davidson

Foxes For Kids
Amazing Animal Books For Young Readers
Zahra Jazeel & John Davidson

Wolves For Kids
Amazing Animal Books For Young Readers
By John Davidson and Virginia Fidler